CHICKEN

Cooking with Style

CASSELL

A CASSELL BOOK

First published in the UK 1994 by Cassell
Villiers House
41/47 Strand
London WC2N 5JE

Copyright © 1994 Weldon Russell Pty Ltd

Produced by Weldon Russell Pty Ltd
107 Union Street, North Sydney, NSW 2060, Australia

A member of the Weldon International Group of Companies

Publisher: Elaine Russell
Publishing manager: Susan Hurley
Editor: Kayte Nunn
Author and home economist: Alexandra McCowan
Designer: Catherine Martin
Photographer: Rowan Fotheringham
Food stylist: Jane Hann
Production: Dianne Leddy

British Library Cataloguing-in-Publication Data
A catalogue record for this book is available from the British Library

ISBN 0-304-34381-1

Printed by Tien Wah Press, Singapore
A KEVIN WELDON PRODUCTION

Acknowledgments: Royal Copenhagen; Waterford Wedgwood; Pillivuyt; Villeroy & Boch; Mikasa; Linen & Lace; Balmain, Sydney.

Cover: *Chicken with Caramelized Apples and Calvados Sauce*
Back cover: *Greek-style Chicken Salad*
Opposite: *Chicken Antipasto Platter* (recipe on page 96)

CONTENTS

Practicalities

Appetizers and Light Meals

Soups

Family Meals

Chicken Satay   46
Chicken Curry with Three Accompaniments   48
"The Works" Mexican Burger   50
Tomato–Basil Spaghettini with Chicken   52

Special Occasions

Chicken with Summer Berry Sauce   54
Chicken with Ginger Sauce and Watermelon Pickle   56
Chicken with Caramelized Apples and Calvados Sauce   58
Basil Chicken with Risotto and Chili–Tomato Coulis   60
Chicken Medallions with Cranberry Glaze   62
Seasoned Chicken Breasts with Creamy Sauce   64
Port, Pear and Fig Casserole   66

Salads & Cold Chicken Dishes

Italian Boned Chicken with Pesto Mayonnaise   68
Warm Chicken and Bell Pepper Salad   70
Greek–style Chicken Salad   72
Chicken and Basil Loaf with Onion–Pepper Relish   74
Smoked Cheese and Chicken Roll   76
Spiced Lime Chicken Salad   78

Roasting, Baking & Barbecuing

Roasted Garlic Chicken with Goat Cheese Bruschetta   80
Creamy Chicken and Leek Pie   82
Chicken with Couscous, Chick Peas and Cumin Sauce   84
Blackened Chicken with Chili–Tomato Coulis   86
Olive–seasoned Chicken with Roasted Tomatoes and Onions   88
Hearty Chicken Casserole with Rye and Raisin Bread   90
Barbecued Cornish Game Hens and Vegetables with Aïoli   92
Wild Rice Seasoned Chicken with Grand Marnier Glaze   94

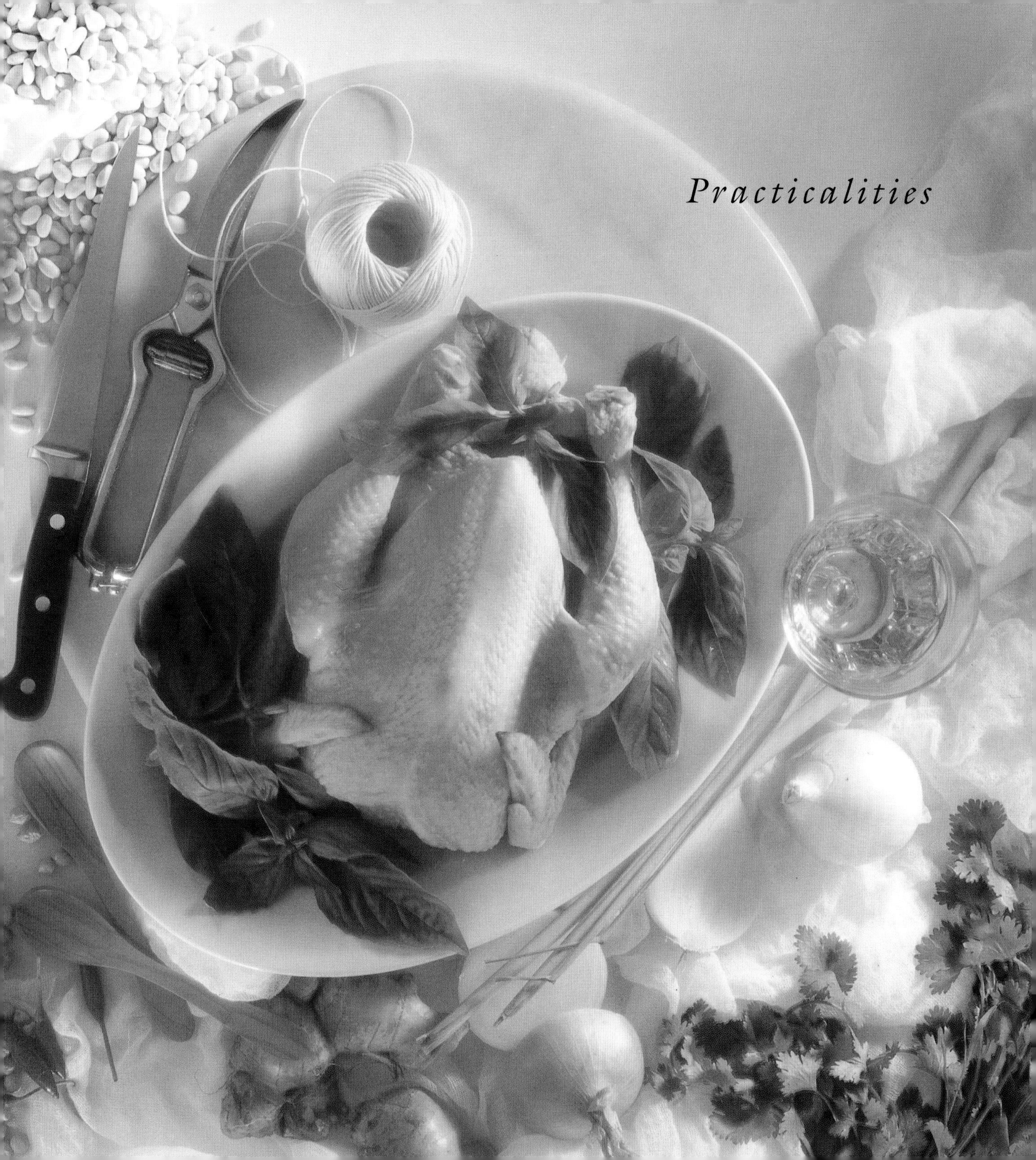

Practicalities

Cutting up a Chicken

A sharp knife and a pair of kitchen shears are required to divide a chicken into pieces.
A chicken can be separated into 9 pieces.

1. Using a sharp knife, remove the thigh and leg section. Separate the leg from the thigh. Repeat with other thigh and leg.

2. Cut the wings from the chicken and then, using poultry shears, separate the breast from the backbone.

3. Using poultry shears, halve the breast section.

4. 8 serving pieces: 2 wings, 2 legs, 2 thighs and 2 breasts. The back can be used in the preparation of stock.

Trussing a Chicken

1. Tie string around the tail end of the chicken and then around the legs.

2. Bring the string between the legs, up to and around the wings.

3. Turn the chicken over and tie the string securely between the wings.

Boning a Chicken

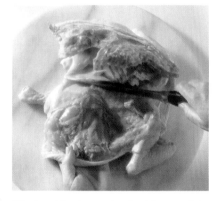

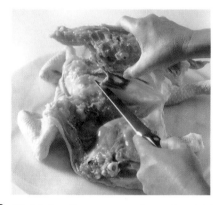

1. Slit the skin down the backbone of the bird. Cut down between the carcass and the flesh on one side of the chicken, easing the flesh away from the bone and cutting through the thigh and wing joints. Repeat the process on the other side of the bird.

2. Hold the rib cage away from the chicken. Carefully remove the rib cage, keeping the knife edge running along the breast bone.

3. Hold the end of the thigh joint in one hand. Work from the inside of the leg and cut away any flesh. Scrape the drumstick until the whole leg bone is free of flesh. Remove the bone.

4. Remove the wing tips at the second joint. Work down the wing bone to the last joint. Pull the bone clear and cut off. Pull the flesh from the legs and wings through to the inside of the bird.

Filling a Chicken

1. Lay the chicken flat, ready for stuffing. Arrange the leg and wing flesh over the flat chicken so it is evenly distributed. Lightly pound the chicken until it is an even thickness.

2. Layer the stuffing ingredients evenly over the chicken according to the particular recipe instructions.

3. Roll up the chicken tightly from the long side, tucking the ends in as you roll.

4. Secure the roll with string at 1 inch (2½ cm) intervals. Join the string ends and secure under the roll.

Crisp Potato Rosti with Chicken

2½ tablespoons vegetable oil

1 onion, chopped

1 clove garlic, crushed

4 large (2 lb/1 kg) potatoes, peeled and coarsely grated

3 tablespoons (1½ oz/45 g) butter

salt and pepper

2 tablespoons corn relish

2 tablespoons salsa (tomato and chili pickle)

1 lb (500 g) cooked chicken, sliced

2 small ripe tomatoes, finely chopped

¼ cup (2 fl oz/60 ml) sour cream

2 tablespoons chopped fresh chives

Heat 1 tablespoon of the oil in a large frying pan, add the onion and garlic and cook, stirring, until the onion is soft. Add the potatoes and cook, stirring, until soft and sticky; cool slightly.

Heat 1½ tablespoons oil and the butter in a clean frying pan. Add one quarter of the potato mixture and press into a round about 6 inches (15 cm) in diameter with a wet spatula. Cook on both sides until well browned and crisp. Remove from the pan, sprinkle with salt and pepper and keep warm. Repeat with the remaining butter–oil mixture and potato mixture.

Combine the corn relish and salsa in a saucepan and stir until heated through. Or, microwave on high (100%) for about 1 minute.

Top the potato rosti with chicken, tomatoes, warm salsa mixture, sour cream and chives and serve immediately.

Serves 4
Preparation/Cooking Time: 1 hour

Thai-style Curried Chicken Skewers

12 skewers
2 lbs (1 kg) boneless, skinless
   chicken breasts
2 tablespoons oil

Curry Paste:
½ onion, chopped
3 cloves garlic, crushed
2 tablespoons chopped fresh lemon
   grass
1 tablespoon chopped fresh
   coriander (cilantro) roots
1 teaspoon chopped fresh chili
   pepper
1 teaspoon grated fresh ginger
1 teaspoon grated lime zest
1 tablespoon Thai fish sauce
1 tablespoon paprika
½ teaspoon cumin seed

2 cups (16 fl oz/500 ml)
   unsweetened coconut milk
1 tablespoon chopped fresh
   coriander (cilantro)

If using bamboo skewers, soak them in water for several hours before using to prevent burning.

Cut the chicken into long, thin strips and thread onto the skewers.

Curry Paste: Blend or process all ingredients until smooth.

Heat the oil in a large shallow pan, add the skewers in batches, and cook on both sides until lightly browned and tender (about 8 minutes); remove from pan. Reheat pan, add the curry paste mixture and cook, stirring, until fragrant (about 2 minutes). Add the coconut milk and coriander (cilantro) and stir until heated through.

Serve the skewers and sauce with jasmine rice, if desired.

Serves 4
Preparation/Cooking Time: 50 minutes

Bitter Greens, Blue Cheese and Chicken Open Sandwiches

3 tablespoons (1½ oz/45 g) butter,
  softened
2 tablespoons sour cream
4 oz (125 g) blue brie, sliced
6 large slices sourdough bread
12 endive leaves
12 chicory leaves
⅓ cup (2½ fl oz/85 ml) olive oil
1 tablespoon lemon juice
1 teaspoon sugar
1 teaspoon grain mustard
8 oz (250 g) cooked chicken, sliced
1 small pear, thinly sliced
½ cup (1¾ oz/50 g) pecans,
  toasted
black pepper

Combine the butter, cream and half the cheese in bowl, beat with a wooden spoon until spreadable. Spread the bread with the cheese mixture.

Combine the endive and chicory leaves with the olive oil, lemon juice, sugar and mustard and toss well. Top the bread with the leaves and dressing, chicken, remaining blue cheese, pear slices and pecans. Sprinkle with freshly ground black pepper and serve immediately.

Makes 6
Preparation Time: 35 minutes

Prosciutto Chicken Frittata

3 tablespoons (1½ oz/45 g) butter

8 (12 oz/375 g) new potatoes,
   thinly sliced

1 red (Spanish) onion, sliced

3 oz (90 g) prosciutto, thinly sliced

10 oz (315 g) cooked chicken,
   shredded

⅓ cup (1½ oz/45 g) drained
   sun-dried tomatoes in oil, sliced

8 eggs, lightly beaten

salt and pepper

½ cup (2 oz/60 g) grated
   Parmesan cheese

1 cup (3 oz/90 g) grated Jarlsberg
   cheese

½ cup (½ oz/15 g) shredded fresh
   basil

Heat 2 tablespoons of the butter in a shallow 10-inch (25-cm) nonstick frying pan. Add the potatoes to the pan and cook, turning occasionally, until golden brown and tender; remove from pan. Heat the remaining butter in the pan, add the onion and prosciutto and cook, stirring, until the onion is soft. Return the potatoes to the pan, mix well and then press the mixture flat in the pan. Top with the tomatoes and chicken.

Combine the eggs, salt and pepper, cheeses and basil and mix well. Gently pour the egg mixture over the chicken mixture in the pan. Cook over a low heat until the base is golden brown (about 10 minutes). Place the pan under a hot broiler (grill) to set and brown the top — cover the pan handle with foil if it is plastic.

Loosen the edges of the frittata, turn onto plate or board and cut into wedges to serve.

This recipe can be made up to a day ahead.

Serves 4 to 6 as an appetizer
Preparation/Cooking Time: 55 minutes

Spicy Chinese-style Chicken Balls

1 lb (500 g) ground (minced)
  chicken
3 cups (6 oz/185 g) stale
  breadcrumbs
1 egg, lightly beaten
4 green (spring) onions, chopped
2 cloves garlic, crushed
2 tablespoons soy sauce
2 tablespoons hoisin sauce
1 teaspoon grated fresh ginger
1 teaspoon sesame oil
2 tablespoons sesame seed
vegetable oil, for deep-frying

Dipping Sauce:
2 tablespoons soy sauce
2 tablespoons sweet chili sauce
1 tablespoon dry sherry

Combine all ingredients except the deep-frying oil in a bowl and mix well. Shape 2 level teaspoons of the mixture into balls. In a deep frying pan, fry the balls in batches in hot oil (350°F/180°C) for about 4 minutes, or until well browned and cooked through — do not have the oil too hot or the balls will not cook through. Drain on paper towels.

Dipping Sauce: Combine all the ingredients in a bowl and mix well.

Serve the hot chicken balls with the dipping sauce.

This recipe can be made a day ahead. Reheat the balls on a baking sheet in a moderate oven (350°F/180°C/Gas 4) for about 10 minutes.

Makes about 70 balls — serves 10 as an hors d'oeuvre
Preparation/Cooking Time: 40 minutes

The Ultimate Chicken Sandwich

2 (6 oz/185 g) jars artichoke
   hearts, drained
1 onion, sliced
2 tablespoons chopped fresh basil
½ cup (2 oz/60 g) drained roasted
   bell peppers (capsicums) in oil,
   sliced
2 tablespoons oil from roasted bell
   peppers (capsicums)
7 oz (220 g) bunch asparagus
   spears
4 boneless, skinless, single chicken
   breasts
4 tablespoons (2 oz/60 g) butter
1 tablespoon olive oil
black pepper
8 slices rye bread, cut ½ inch
   (1.25 cm) thick
1 bunch (4 oz/120 g) arugula
   (rocket), washed and stemmed

Dijon Mayonnaise:
⅓ cup (3 fl oz/90 ml) mayonnaise
1 tablespoon Dijon mustard
¼ teaspoon Tabasco sauce
salt and pepper

Combine the artichoke hearts, onion, basil, bell peppers (capsicums) and oil in a bowl and toss well.

Boil, steam or microwave the asparagus until just tender and drain.

Pound the chicken breasts until thin, cut in half crosswise.

Heat 2 tablespoons of the butter and the oil in a frying pan, add the chicken, sprinkle with black pepper, and cook over a high heat until the chicken is tender (about 3 minutes).

Dijon Mayonnaise: Combine all the ingredients in a bowl and mix well.

Spread the bread slices with the remaining 2 tablespoons of butter and top half the bread slices with the arugula (rocket) leaves, half the chicken, asparagus, artichoke mixture and Dijon mayonnaise; top with the remaining chicken and bread slices. Serve while still warm.

Serves 4
Preparation/Cooking Time: 25 minutes

Japanese–style Skewers

12 skewers
1½ lb (750 g) boneless, skinless,
  single chicken breasts
¼ cup (2 fl oz/60 ml) bottled
  teriyaki sauce
1 tablespoon mirin
2 cloves garlic, crushed
2 teaspoons grated fresh ginger
vegetable oil for shallow-frying
1 teaspoon sugar
½ cup (2 oz/60 g) cornstarch
  (cornflour)

Dipping Sauce:
1½ tablespoons soy sauce
1 tablespoon mirin
1 teaspoon sugar
½ teaspoon sesame oil
1 teaspoon sesame seeds

If using bamboo skewers, soak them in water for at least 1 hour before using, to prevent burning.

Cut the chicken into strips and thread onto the skewers. Place the skewers in a shallow nonmetallic dish and pour over combined teriyaki sauce, mirin, garlic, ginger and sugar. Cover and refrigerate for several hours or overnight.

Drain the skewers from the marinade, and discard marinade. Heat about 1½ inches (4 cm) of oil in a frying pan. Toss the skewers in cornstarch (cornflour) and shallow-fry in the oil until well browned and tender. Drain on paper towels. Serve the chicken skewers with the Dipping Sauce.

Dipping Sauce: Combine all ingredients in a bowl and mix well.

Mirin is a sweet rice wine used in Japanese cooking and available from Asian grocers. You can substitute dry sherry if mirin is unavailable. The uncooked marinated skewers can be frozen.

Serves 4
Preparation/Cooking Time: 35 minutes
Marinating Time: Several hours

Thai-style Chicken and Coconut Soup

2 tablespoons vegetable oil

2 onions, chopped

3 cloves garlic, crushed

2 teaspoons ground cumin

1 teaspoon turmeric

1 teaspoon chopped fresh chili pepper

1 tablespoon chopped fresh lemon grass*

¼ cup (2 fl oz/60 ml) lime juice

4 cups (32 fl oz/1 l) chicken stock

2 cups (16 fl oz/500 ml) unsweetened coconut cream

2 tablespoons Thai fish sauce**

1 lb (500g) boneless, skinless chicken breasts, thinly sliced

2 tablespoons chopped fresh coriander (cilantro)

lime leaves, for garnish

*Lemon grass is available from Asian food stores. If lemon grass is unavailable, substitute 2 teaspoons grated lime zest.

**Fish sauce is also available from Asian food stores. If unavailable, substitute light soy sauce.

Heat the oil in a frying pan, add the onion and garlic and cook, stirring, until the onion is soft. Add the spices, chili and lemon grass and cook, stirring, until the lemon grass is tender. Add the lime juice, stock, coconut cream and fish sauce and bring to a boil. Stir in the chicken and simmer, uncovered, for about 3 minutes, or until the chicken is tender. Stir in the remaining ingredients and cook until hot.

This recipe can be made a day ahead.

Serves 4 as a main course — 8 as an appetizer
Preparation/Cooking Time: 35 minutes

Hearty Chicken Soup with Dumplings

½ cup (4 oz/125 g) pearl barley

½ lb (250 g) frozen lima (broad) beans

2 tablespoons oil

2 lbs (1 kg) boneless, skinless chicken breasts, sliced

3 leeks, well-washed, trimmed and sliced

2 cloves garlic, crushed

3 stalks celery, chopped

3 medium carrots, chopped

2 medium zucchinis (courgettes), chopped

8 cups (64 fl oz/2 l) chicken stock

½ cup (2 fl oz/60 ml) tomato paste

⅓ cup (½ oz/15 g) chopped fresh parsley

1 tablespoon chopped fresh thyme

salt and pepper

Dumplings:

¼ cup (1½ oz/45 g) cornmeal

¾ cup (3½ oz/100 g) all-purpose (plain) flour

1½ teaspoons baking powder

¼ teaspoon salt

½ cup (1½ oz/45 g) grated Parmesan cheese

4 tablespoons (2 oz/60 g) cold butter, grated

½ cup (4 fl oz/125 ml)

Rinse the barley under cold water until the water runs clear; drain. Pour boiling water over the beans, drain and remove skins.

Heat the oil in a large saucepan, add the chicken in batches, cook until well browned all over — this is important to achieve color and flavor. Add the leeks, garlic, celery, carrots and zucchini, cook, stirring, until leeks are soft. Add the chicken stock and tomato paste, bring to a boil. Add the barley and simmer, covered, for 20 minutes. Return the chicken to the pan with the beans.

Dumplings: Combine the dry ingredients in a bowl, stir in the cheese and butter and mix well. Add enough of the water to form a soft dough. Drop level tablespoons of dumpling mixture into the simmering soup, cover and simmer for about 15 minutes, or until the dumplings are cooked through and the barley is tender. Stir in the herbs, season to taste with salt and pepper, serve immediately.

The soup can be prepared a day ahead, however, the barley will thicken the soup overnight. The dumplings are best made just before serving as they will thicken soup also.

Serves 6
Preparation/Cooking Time: 1 hour 25 minutes

Oriental Broth with Chicken Wings

6 dried Chinese mushrooms

Chinese Chicken Stock:
3 lbs (1.5 kg) chicken bones
16 cups (128 fl oz/4 l) cold water
1 (2 in/5 cm) piece fresh ginger,
  sliced
6 green (spring) onions, chopped
1 teaspoon black peppercorns

4 chicken wings
1 (2 in/5 cm) piece fresh ginger,
  cut into julienne
1 leek, well-washed, trimmed and
  thinly sliced
1 carrot, thinly sliced
4 green (spring) onions, sliced
  diagonally
¼ cup (2 fl oz/60 ml)
  reduced-sodium soy sauce
1 teaspoon sesame oil
1 teaspoon chopped fresh chili
  pepper

Pour boiling water over the mushrooms in a bowl and leave to stand for 20 minutes. Drain and slice mushrooms thinly.
Chinese Chicken Stock: Combine all the ingredients in a large saucepan, bring to a boil. Skim the surface, reduce the heat and simmer, uncovered, for 3 hours. Strain and then cool. Refrigerate for several hours or overnight and then skim the fat from the surface. Return the stock to the pan and boil, uncovered, until the stock is reduced to 5 cups.

Combine the stock and wings in a large pan, bring to a boil and simmer, covered, for 10 minutes. Add the vegetables and simmer, covered, for a further 5 minutes, or until the chicken wings are tender. Add the soy sauce, sesame oil and chili and stir until hot. Place 1 wing in each serving bowl, ladle the broth and vegetables over the wings.

A low-salt, purchased chicken stock can be used for convenience in this recipe.

Serves 4 as an appetizer
Preparation/Cooking Time: 45 minutes

Chicken and Corn Soup with Cornmeal Muffins

Cornmeal Muffins:

1 cup (6 oz/185 g) yellow cornmeal (polenta)

½ cup (2 oz/60 g) all-purpose (plain) flour

1½ teaspoons baking powder

2 teaspoons sugar

½ teaspoon salt

2 eggs, lightly beaten

½ cup (4 fl oz/125 ml) buttermilk

6 tablespoons (3 oz/90g) butter

1 (4½ oz/140 g) can corn kernels

¾ cup (3 oz/90 g) grated cheese

1½ tablespoons vegetable oil

5 oz (155 g) chorizo sausage

4 boneless single chicken breasts

2 onions, chopped

2 cloves garlic, crushed

1 tablespoon ground cumin

3 cups (24 fl oz/750 ml) stock

3 cups (24 fl oz/750 ml) tomato juice

2½ tablespoons tomato paste

2 red bell peppers (capsicum)

2 zucchini (courgettes)

1 can (12 oz/375 g) kidney beans

1 can (12 oz/375 g) corn kernels

2½ tablespoons coriander (cilantro)

Cornmeal Muffins: Combine the dry ingredients in a bowl, melt the butter and drain the corn kernels. Stir in with the remaining ingredients and mix well. Spoon the mixture into 8 greased muffin cups (⅓ cup capacity each). Bake at 400°F (200°C/ Gas 6) for 25 minutes, or until cooked when tested with skewer. While the muffins are baking, prepare the soup.

Heat the oil in a large pan. Chop the chorizo and slice the chicken. Add in batches and cook, stirring, until lightly browned; remove from pan. Reheat the pan, add the onions and garlic and cook, stirring, until the onions soften. Add the cumin and cook, stirring, until the spices are fragrant (about 1 minute). Add the stock, tomato juice and tomato paste and bring to a boil. Chop the bell peppers (capsicums) and zucchini (courgettes) and add. Simmer, uncovered, for about 5 minutes or until just tender. Stir in the chicken, rinsed and drained kidney beans, drained corn and coriander (cilantro) and simmer, uncovered, until hot. Serve with the Cornmeal Muffins.

The soup can be made a day ahead. The Cornmeal Muffins are suitable for freezing.

Serves 4 as a main course or 8 as an appetizer
Preparation/Cooking Time: 1 hour

Chicken and Saffron Bouillabaisse

¼ cup (2 fl oz/60 ml) olive oil

2 leeks, well-washed, trimmed and sliced

2 cloves garlic, crushed

4 chicken legs, skin removed

6 large sticks celery, thickly sliced

1 (14 oz/440 g) can tomatoes, undrained, crushed

⅓ cup (2½ fl oz/75 ml) Pernod or Ricard

¼ teaspoon powdered saffron or saffron threads

1 tablespoon chopped fresh thyme

2 tablespoons chopped fresh dill

3 cups (24 fl oz/750 ml) chicken stock

Tabasco sauce

salt and pepper

Combine all of the ingredients except the stock, Tabasco sauce and salt and pepper in large nonmetallic dish. Stir well to coat the chicken in the liquid. Cover and refrigerate overnight.

Pour chicken and marinade into a large saucepan, bring to a boil. Then cover and simmer for 15 minutes. Add the chicken stock and simmer, covered, for a further 15 minutes, or until chicken is tender. Season to taste with Tabasco and salt and pepper before serving.

This recipe is best if prepared a day ahead and reheated gently just before serving.

Serves 4
Preparation/Cooking Time: 50 minutes
Marinating Time: Overnight

Cumin Pancake Stacks
with Chicken and Guacamole

2 red bell peppers (capsicums)
4 bacon strips (rashers), halved,
  rind removed
2 ripe avocados
2 tablespoons chopped fresh
  coriander (cilantro)
1 tablespoon taco (chili) sauce
2 teaspoons lime juice
salt and pepper
1 lb (500 g) cooked chicken, sliced
2 tomatoes, chopped
taco (chili) sauce, extra
⅓ cup (3 fl oz/90 ml) sour cream
1 tablespoon packed fresh
  coriander (cilantro) leaves

Cumin Pancakes:
1 teaspoon cumin seed
2 cups (10 oz/315 g) all purpose
  (plain) flour
1 teaspoon baking soda
  (bicarbonate of soda)
1 tablespoon sugar
3 eggs, separated
2 cups (16 fl oz/500 ml)
  buttermilk
4 tablespoons (2 oz/60 g) butter,
  melted
1 (12 oz/375 g) can corn kernels,
  drained

Quarter the bell peppers (capsicums) and remove the seeds and membrane. Broil (grill) the peppers, skin side up, until skin blisters and blackens (about 10 minutes). Peel the skin and slice thinly.

Cumin Pancakes: Toast the cumin seed in a dry frying pan until fragrant (about 2 minutes). Sift the flour, baking soda and sugar into bowl. Combine the egg yolks, buttermilk and butter and whisk into flour, soda and sugar mixture until smooth. Stir in the corn kernels and cumin seed. (Or, blend the above ingredients, except the corn, in a food processor until smooth. Then stir in the corn.)

Beat the egg whites in a small bowl with an electric mixer until soft peaks form. Fold into the batter in two batches.

Pour ½ cup of the mixture into a heated greased frying pan and cook until golden brown underneath and bubbles begin to burst on top. Turn the pancakes and cook until browned and set. Remove from the pan and keep warm. Repeat with the remaining pancake batter. You will need 12 pancakes for this recipe.

Place the bacon in a dry frying pan and cook until just crisp.

Combine the avocados, chopped coriander (cilantro), taco (chili) sauce and lime juice in a bowl and mash well with a fork; season to taste with salt and pepper.

Place one pancake on each plate, top with some of the avocado mixture, chicken, pepper, bacon and chopped tomatoes; drizzle with the extra taco (chili) sauce. Repeat, making another layer and topping it with a pancake layer. Top with sour cream and coriander (cilantro), if desired. Assemble the remaining 3 servings.

The pancakes are best made close to serving. The filling can be prepared up to a day ahead and reheated before serving.

Serves 4
Preparation/Cooking Time: 1 hour

Hoisin Noodle Stir-fry

Marinade:

⅓ cup (3 fl oz/90 ml) hoisin sauce

2 cloves garlic, crushed

2 tablespoons dry sherry

1 tablespoon honey

2 tablespoons soy sauce

¼ teaspoon Chinese five-spice
   powder

4 boneless, skinless, single chicken
   breasts, thinly sliced

1 lb (500 g) package fresh thick
   egg noodles

2 tablespoons oil

2 onions, sliced lengthwise

2 cloves garlic, crushed

4 bunches (4 lbs/2 kg) bok choy,
   washed

1 red bell pepper (capsicum),
   thinly sliced

1 green bell pepper (capsicum),
   thinly sliced

1 yellow pepper (capsicum), thinly
   sliced

1 tablespoon cornstarch
   (cornflour)

2 tablespoons cold water

Combine all the marinade ingredients and the chicken in a dish and mix well. Cover and refrigerate for several hours or overnight. Drain the chicken from the marinade, reserve marinade.

Add the noodles to a pan of boiling water and simmer, uncovered for 3 minutes; drain.

Heat the oil in a wok or large pan, add the chicken in batches and cook, stirring, until the chicken is browned and tender; remove from the wok. Reheat the wok, add the onions and garlic and cook, stirring, until the onion is soft. Add the bok choy and bell peppers (capsicums) and cook, stirring, until the bok choy is wilted. Add the noodles, toss well and then transfer to serving plates.

Blend the reserved marinade with the cornstarch (cornflour) and water. Add to the wok and cook, stirring, until the mixture boils and thickens. Return the chicken to the wok and stir-fry until heated through. Spoon onto the bok choy mixture on the serving plates.

This recipe can be prepared a day ahead. Fresh egg noodles are available from Asian supermarkets. If using dried noodles, boil them first until tender.

Serves 4
Preparation/Cooking Time: 45 minutes
Marinating Time: Several hours

Creamy Chicken and Mushroom Filo Parcels

Filling:

2 tablespoons (1 oz/30 g) butter

2 bacon strips (rashers), chopped

5 oz (155 g) small white (button) mushrooms, chopped

5 oz (155 g) field (flat) mushrooms, chopped

6 green (spring) onions, chopped

1 tablespoon grain mustard

4 oz (125 g) cream cheese, chopped

⅓ cup (2½ fl oz/80 ml) heavy (whipping) cream

1 lb (500 g) cooked chicken chopped

10 sheets filo pastry

4 tablespoons (2 oz/60 g) butter, melted

2 teaspoons poppy seeds

Filling: Heat the butter in a frying pan, add the bacon and mushrooms and cook, stirring, until the liquid has evaporated. Add the green (spring) onions and cook, stirring, until soft. Stir in the mustard, cream cheese, cream and chicken and mix well.

Layer 5 sheets of filo pastry together, brushing each layer with melted butter. Keep the unused pastry covered with a barely damp, clean dish towel at all times to prevent drying out. Cut the pastry in half to form two squares. Spoon one fourth of the filling onto the end of each square, roll once, tuck the ends in and roll up. Brush lightly with butter and then sprinkle with poppy seeds. Repeat with the remaining pastry and filling.

Place on a lightly greased baking sheet. Bake at 400°F (200°C/ Gas 6) for about 20 minutes or, until lightly browned and filling is hot.

The parcels can be prepared a day ahead. Store, covered with plastic wrap, in refrigerator.

Serves 4
Preparation/Cooking Time: 50 minutes

Baked Chicken and Pumpkin Slice with Herbed Cream Sauce

3 cups cooked mashed pumpkin

1 lb (500 g) cooked chicken, finely
   chopped

8 tablespoons (4 oz/125 g) butter,
   melted

1 cup (6 oz/185 g) semolina flour

½ cup (4½ oz/140 g) ricotta
   cheese

½ cup (1¾ oz/50 g) grated
   Parmesan cheese

6 green (spring) onions, chopped

2 cloves garlic, crushed

5 eggs, lightly beaten

salt and pepper

Herbed Cream Sauce:

2 teaspoons olive oil

4 cloves garlic, crushed

½ cup (4 fl oz/125 ml) dry white
   wine

½ cup (4 fl oz/125 ml) chicken
   stock

1 cup (8 fl oz/250 ml) heavy
   (whipping) cream

2 tablespoons chopped fresh basil

2 tablespoons chopped fresh
   oregano

2 tablespoons chopped fresh chives

salt and white pepper

Combine all the Baked Chicken and Pumpkin Slice ingredients in a large bowl, season with salt and pepper and mix well. Lightly grease a 3 x 9 inch (30 x 25 cm) baking dish. Spread the mixture evenly into the prepared dish and smooth over the top. Bake at 400°F (200°C/Gas 6) for about 40 minutes, or until firm. *Herbed Cream Sauce:* While the chicken and pumpkin mixture is baking, heat the oil in a small saucepan, add the garlic and cook, stirring, until the garlic is lightly browned. Add the wine and stock and simmer, uncovered, until reduced to about ½ cup. Add the cream and herbs and stir until hot; season with salt and white pepper.

Cut the baked chicken and pumpkin mixture into small diamond shapes, divide between warmed serving dishes and spoon over the Herbed Cream Sauce.

This recipe can be made a day ahead and kept covered, separately, in the refrigerator. The baked chicken and pumpkin mixture is suitable for freezing.

Serves 6
Preparation/Cooking Time: 1 hour

Chicken, Oyster Mushroom and Artichoke Pizza

2 green bell peppers (capsicums)
2 tablespoons olive oil
2 onions, sliced
2 cloves garlic, crushed
10 oz (315 g) oyster mushrooms, halved
2 x 15 oz (470 g) prepared pizza bases
⅓ cup (3 fl oz/90 ml) tomato paste
1 tablespoon extra virgin olive oil
2 tablespoons chopped fresh basil
1 lb (500 g) mozzarella cheese, grated
1 lb (500 g) cooked chicken, sliced
2 (6 oz/185 g) jars marinated artichoke hearts, drained
⅓ cup (1 oz/30 g) drained sun-dried tomatoes in oil, sliced
⅓ cup (2½ oz/75 g) drained black (Riviera) olives
freshly ground black pepper
extra olive oil, if desired

Quarter the bell peppers and remove seeds and membranes. Broil (grill) the peppers, skin side up, until skin blisters and blackens. Peel the skin and slice thinly.

Heat the oil in a frying pan, add the onions, garlic and mushrooms and cook, stirring, until the onions are soft.

Place the pizza bases on baking sheets and spread with combined tomato paste, olive oil and basil. Top with half the cheese then the chicken, artichokes, mushroom mixture, bell peppers, tomatoes and olives; top with remaining cheese. Sprinkle with freshly ground black pepper and drizzle with extra olive oil, if desired. Bake at 500°F (250°C/Gas 10) for about 15 minutes, or until well browned and hot.

This recipe can be prepared a day ahead — assemble just before serving.

Serves 4 to 6
Preparation/Cooking Time: 40 minutes

Chicken Curry with Three Accompaniments

1/4 cup (2 oz/60 g) ghee
2 lbs (1 kg) boneless, skinless
  chicken breasts, sliced
2 onions, chopped
3 cloves garlic, crushed
2 teaspoons grated fresh ginger
1 tablespoon curry powder
1 teaspoon turmeric
2 teaspoons ground cumin
1 teaspoon garam masala
1/2 teaspoon chopped fresh chili
1 (13 oz/410 g) can tomatoes
1 cup (8 fl oz/250 ml) stock
2 cups (16 fl oz/500 ml)
  unsweetened coconut cream
1 green bell pepper (capsicum)
8 oz (250 g) cauliflower
3 Oriental (lady finger) eggplants
1 tablespoon chopped fresh
  coriander (cilantro)
1 sheet store-bought puff pastry
1 teaspoon milk

Three Accompaniments:
1 small green cucumber
1/2 cup (4 fl oz/125 ml) yogurt
1 tablespoon chopped fresh mint
1 tablespoon coriander (cilantro)
2 small tomatoes, finely chopped
1 tablespoon lime juice
1/3 cup (3 1/2 oz/100 g) chutney

Heat 3 tablespoons of the ghee in a large frying pan, add the chicken in batches and cook, stirring, over a high heat until the chicken is golden brown; remove from the pan.

Reheat the pan with the remaining ghee, add the onions, garlic, ginger, spices and chili and cook, stirring, until the onion is soft and the spices are fragrant. Add the undrained tomatoes, stock and coconut cream and bring to a boil. Chop the vegetables and add. Simmer, uncovered, for about 20 minutes, or until the vegetables are tender and the sauce is thickened. Return the chicken to the pan and simmer until the chicken is tender. Stir in the coriander (cilantro).

You will need 4 ovenproof 2-cup-capacity serving dishes. Cut 4 rounds of pastry large enough to fit the tops of the dishes. Divide the curry mixture among the dishes. Lay the pastry on top of the dishes and brush lightly with the milk. Place the dishes on a baking sheet and bake at 450°F (230°C/Gas 8) for about 10 minutes, or until the pastry is well puffed and golden brown.

Three Accompaniments: Finely chop the cucumber, combine with the yogurt and mint and mix well. Chop the coriander and combine with the tomatoes and lime juice in a bowl. Mix well.

Serve the yogurt mixture, tomato mixture and chutney in separate bowls.

Serve the chicken curry immediately with the three accompaniments.

The curry and accompaniments can be made a day ahead. Reheat the curry in a pan until hot before topping with pastry and completing.

Ghee is clarified butter.

Serves 4
Preparation/Cooking Time: 1 hour 15 minutes

"The Works" Mexican Burger

2 tablespoons vegetable oil
2 onions, sliced
½ teaspoon ground cumin
1 large avocado
2 teaspoons lime juice
salt and pepper
1 (15 oz/470 g) can refried beans
6½ oz (200 g) packet corn chips
½ head romaine (cos) lettuce,
   shredded
1 cup (8 fl oz/250 ml) prepared
   chunky-style salsa
⅓ cup (3 fl oz/90 ml) sour cream
fresh coriander (cilantro) sprigs
⅓ cup (3 fl oz/90 ml) chili sauce

Burgers:
1½ lb (750 g) ground (minced)
   chicken
1 tablespoon chopped fresh
   coriander
1 tablespoon ground cumin
1 teaspoon salt
¼ teaspoon chili powder
2 cloves garlic, crushed
6 green (spring) onions, chopped
2½ cups (5 oz/155 g) stale
   breadcrumbs
1 egg, lightly beaten
2 tablespoons vegetable oil

Heat the oil in frying pan, add the onions and cook, stirring, until the onions are soft. Add the cumin and cook, stirring, until fragrant.

Mash the avocado with lime juice and salt and pepper to taste — keep tightly covered.

Heat the refried beans in a saucepan or microwave on high (100%) for about 3 minutes.

Burgers: Combine chicken, coriander, cumin, salt, chili powder, garlic, green (spring) onions, 1½ cups of the breadcrumbs and the egg in a bowl and mix well. Shape the mixture into 4 large flat patties, about 1 inch (2.5 cm) thick. Press the remaining cup of breadcrumbs onto the patties and refrigerate for 1 hour.

Heat the oil in a large shallow frying pan and cook the burger patties over a medium–low heat until they are well browned and cooked through (about 5 minutes on each side).

Arrange the corn chips around the edge of the plates, pile the lettuce in the center. Top with a burger, then some of the beans, onions, salsa, avocado, sour cream and coriander (cilantro); drizzle with the chili sauce.

This recipe can be prepared a day ahead — reheat and assemble just before serving. The uncooked patties are suitable for freezing.

Stale breadcrumbs are made from 1–2 day-old bread — do not substitute dried packaged breadcrumbs. Stale breadcrumbs can be made in large quantities in the food processor and frozen in 1 cup bags for convenience.

Serves 4
Preparation/Cooking Time: 50 minutes

Tomato–Basil Spaghettini with Chicken

2 tablespoons olive oil

5 oz (155 g) prosciutto, sliced

4 boneless, skinless, single chicken
   breasts, sliced into thick strips

1 tablespoon balsamic vinegar

Tomato–Basil Spaghettini:

1 lb (500 g) spaghettini

1 tablespoon extra virgin olive oil

2 cloves garlic, crushed

6 (approx. 3 lbs/1.3 kg) large ripe
   tomatoes, peeled and finely
   chopped

⅓ cup (⅓ oz/10 g) chopped fresh
   basil

5 oz (155 g) bocconcini, cubed

½ cup (1¾ oz/50 g) grated
   Parmesan cheese

2 teaspoons sugar

¼ cup (1 oz/30 g) drained
   sun-dried tomatoes, sliced

salt and pepper

Heat the oil in a frying pan, add the prosciutto and cook until just crisp; drain. Reheat the pan and add the chicken. Cook, stirring, until the chicken is just tender. Add the balsamic vinegar to the pan and stir until well coated.

Tomato–Basil Spaghettini: Add the pasta to a large pan of boiling water and boil uncovered, until just tender. Drain and keep warm.

Heat the oil in a saucepan, add the garlic, tomatoes and basil and simmer, uncovered, for about 10 minutes, or until mixture has become pulpy. Stir in the cheeses, sugar and sun-dried tomatoes; season to taste with salt and pepper, and toss through the spaghettini.

Serve the Tomato–Basil Spaghettini with the chicken and prosciutto, top with Parmesan cheese and shredded basil.

Bocconcini are small fresh mozzarella balls available from gourmet delicatessens. Substitute mozzarella if unavailable.

Serves 4
Preparation/Cooking Time: 45 minutes

Chicken with Summer Berry Sauce

1 (3 lb/1.5 kg) chicken

2 tablespoons (1 oz/30 g) butter, melted

salt and pepper

3 tablespoons raspberry jam

3 tablespoons red wine vinegar

⅔ cup (5 fl oz/155 ml) dry white wine

1 teaspoon cornstarch (cornflour)

½ cup (4 fl oz/125 ml) orange juice

3 oz (90 g) fresh or frozen blueberries

3 oz (90 g) fresh or frozen raspberries

3 oz (90 g) fresh or frozen blackberries*

¼ cup (2 fl oz/60 ml) Grand Marnier liqueur

*Substitute any summer berries if these are unavailable. If using frozen berries, allow to thaw and drain well before using.

Cut the chicken along either side of the backbone, using poultry shears or a sharp knife, discard backbone. Cut through the center of the breast bone, then cut each half in half crosswise. Place the chicken in a baking dish, brush with butter and sprinkle with salt and pepper. Bake at 400°F (200°C/Gas 6) for about 30 minutes, or until tender. While the chicken is baking, prepare the sauce.

Combine the jam, vinegar and wine in a saucepan and stir until the jam dissolves. Boil, uncovered, until reduced to about ½ a cup. Strain.

Blend the cornstarch (cornflour) and orange juice and stir into the mixture; cook until the mixture boils and thickens. Just before serving, add the berries and simmer gently, without stirring, until the berries are heated through. Gently warm the Grand Marnier in a small saucepan over low heat. Ignite carefully, pour over the sauce in the pan. Serve with the chicken.

The sauce can be prepared a day ahead. Finish off the sauce just before serving.

The chicken can also be char-grilled or barbecued slowly in a covered barbecue until tender.

Serves 4
Preparation/Cooking Time: 40 minutes

Chicken with Ginger Sauce and Watermelon Pickle

Watermelon Pickle:

1 small (3 lb 10 oz/1.8 kg)
  watermelon

1 cinnamon stick

½ cup (4 fl oz/125 ml) white
  vinegar

2 teaspoons grated fresh ginger

1 onion, chopped

¼ cup (2 oz/60 g) superfine
  (caster) sugar

2 tablespoons vegetable oil

6 boneless, skinless, single chicken
  breasts

¾ cup (6 fl oz/185 ml) dry white
  wine

1 cup (8 fl oz/250 ml) chicken
  stock

2 tablespoons grated fresh ginger

4 tablespoons (2 oz/60 g) cold
  butter, cubed

2 teaspoons cornstarch (cornflour)

2 teaspoons cold water

Watermelon Pickle: Remove the seeds and rind from the watermelon; finely chop the flesh. Combine the watermelon with remaining pickle ingredients in a saucepan. Bring to a boil and boil rapidly, uncovered, for about 20 minutes, or until most of the liquid has evaporated. Discard the cinnamon stick. If storing, pour into a hot sterilized jar, cool and refrigerate. Use at room temperature. Reserve 2 tablespoons of pickle juice.

Heat the oil in a frying pan, add the chicken and cook until well browned and tender. Remove chicken from pan and keep warm.

Drain any excess fat from the pan. Add the wine and stock to the pan and bring to a boil. Reduce the heat and simmer, uncovered, until the liquid has reduced to about 1 cup.

Press the grated ginger between two spoons to extract the juice, discard the pulp. Add the ginger juice and 2 tablespoons of juice from the watermelon pickle to the pan. Whisk in the butter over low heat, one piece at a time, until combined. Blend the cornstarch (cornflour) and water and add to the mixture. Stir until mixture boils and thickens.

Cut the chicken into slices. Divide the sauce between plates, serve with sliced chicken and Watermelon Pickle.

The Watermelon Pickle can be made up to a month ahead and stored in a sterilized jar in the refrigerator. The chicken and sauce are best made close to serving.

Serves 6
Preparation/Cooking Time: 1 hour

Chicken with Caramelized Apples and Calvados Sauce

1 tablespoon vegetable oil

4 boneless, skinless, single chicken breasts

3 tablespoons (1½ oz/45 g) butter

2 tablespoons packed brown sugar

2 small apples, peeled and sliced

1 cup (8 fl oz/250 ml) clear apple juice

½ cup (4 fl oz/125 ml) chicken stock

1 tablespoon cornstarch (cornflour)

1 tablespoon cold water

¼ cup (2 fl oz/60 ml) heavy (whipping) cream

1 tablespoon fresh chervil sprigs (or chives)

2 tablespoons Calvados or brandy

Heat the oil in a frying pan, add the chicken and cook until well browned and tender. Remove from the pan and keep warm.

Drain any excess oil from the pan. Heat the butter and sugar in the pan, add the apples, and cook until the apples are lightly browned; remove apples from pan with a slotted spoon. Add the apple juice to the pan and simmer until reduced by about one third. Add the stock and blended cornstarch (cornflour) and water and stir constantly until the mixture boils and thickens. Stir in the cream, chervil and apples.

Heat the Calvados gently in a small saucepan over a low heat. Ignite carefully, and pour over the sauce. Serve the chicken with the sauce immediately.

Serves 4
Preparation/Cooking Time: 40 minutes

Basil Chicken with Risotto and Chili–Tomato Coulis

Chili–Tomato Coulis:

1 tablespoon olive oil
1 onion, chopped
1 clove garlic, crushed
1 (28 oz/880 g) can plum tomatoes
1 tablespoon tomato paste
1½ tablespoons sweet chili sauce

Risotto:

2 tablespoons olive oil
1 large onion, chopped
1 clove garlic, crushed
1½ cups arborio rice
pinch saffron or ¼ teaspoon turmeric
½ cup (4 fl oz/125 ml) dry white wine
4 cups (32 fl oz/1 l) hot chicken stock
3 tablespoons (1½ oz/45 g) butter
⅓ cup (1 oz/30 g) grated Parmesan cheese

2 tablespoons olive oil
6 skinless, boneless, single chicken breasts
2 tablespoons (1 oz/30 g) butter
2 tablespoons chopped fresh basil

Chili–Tomato Coulis: Heat the oil in a saucepan, add the onion and garlic and cook, stirring, until the onion is soft. Add the undrained tomatoes and simmer, uncovered, until pulpy (about 5 minutes). Blend or process the mixture until just smooth — do not over-process or the sauce will become orange rather than red. Press the mixture through a sieve; discard the pulp. Stir in the tomato paste and sweet chili sauce and simmer, uncovered, until the mixture has reduced to about 2 cups. Season with salt and pepper.

Risotto: Heat the oil in a saucepan, add the onion and garlic and cook, stirring, until the onion is soft. Add the rice and saffron and stir until the rice is well coated. Add the wine and ¼ cup of hot stock. Simmer, stirring until all of the liquid is absorbed. Add the remaining stock in about 4 batches, stirring until the liquid is absorbed before adding more stock. Cooking time should be about 20 minutes, or until the rice is tender. Finally, stir in the butter and cheese.

Heat the oil in a frying pan, add the chicken and cook until well browned and tender. Slice the chicken diagonally and return to the pan with the butter and basil, stir until well combined.

Divide the Chili–Tomato Coulis between the plates, top with the Risotto and the chicken mixture.

Arborio rice is a large, Italian, round-grained rice, suitable for risotto. Other types of short-grain white rice can be substituted. The chicken can be cooked and sliced a day ahead — toss in butter and basil when reheating. The Chili–Tomato Coulis can be made a day ahead. The Risotto is best made close to serving.

Serves 6
Preparation/Cooking Time: 1 hour

Chicken Medallions with Cranberry Glaze

4 boneless, skinless, single chicken
  breasts
handful all-purpose (plain) flour
2 tablespoons vegetable oil
black pepper
1 cup (8 fl oz/250 ml) chicken
  stock
1 cup (8 fl oz/250 ml) port
¼ cup (2¾ oz/80 g) cranberry
  sauce
⅓ cup (1¾ oz/50 g) fresh or
  frozen cranberries

Cut each chicken breast into four diagonal slices. Pound each slice into a thin oval shape. Toss the chicken in flour; shake away any excess flour.

Heat the oil in a frying pan, add the chicken pieces in two batches, sprinkle with black pepper and cook over high heat until well browned and tender. Remove the chicken from the pan and keep warm.

Drain any excess fat from the pan and then add the chicken stock and port and simmer, uncovered, until reduced to about 1 cup. Stir in the cranberry sauce and cranberries until heated through.

Serve immediately with the chicken.

Serves 4
Preparation/Cooking Time: 25 minutes

Seasoned Chicken Breasts with Creamy Sauce

4 boneless, skinless, single chicken
  breasts
3 tablespoons (1½ oz/45 g) butter
2 bacon strips (rashers), chopped
2 leeks, well-washed, trimmed and
  finely chopped
1 clove garlic, crushed
⅓ cup (1½ oz/45 g) drained
  sun-dried tomatoes, finely
  chopped
¼ cup (1 oz/30 g) grated
  Parmesan cheese
2 teaspoons grain mustard
2 tablespoons plus 2 teaspoons
  chopped fresh basil
1 tablespoon plus 2 teaspoons
  vegetable oil
½ cup (4 fl oz/125 ml) dry white
  wine
½ cup (4 fl oz/125 ml) chicken
  stock
½ cup (4 fl oz/125 ml) heavy
  (whipping) cream
1 teaspoon cornstarch (cornflour)
1 teaspoon cold water
toothpicks for securing

Remove the tenderloin (supreme) from the chicken breast. Remove the white sinew from tenderloins and then process the tenderloins until finely minced.

Heat the butter in a frying pan, add the bacon, leeks and garlic and cook, stirring, until the leeks are soft; add the sun-dried tomatoes and mix well. Reserve ¼ cup of the mixture for the sauce. Combine the remaining mixture with the cheese, mustard, 2 tablespoons of the basil and the minced chicken; mix well.

Cut a pocket in one side of each chicken breast, taking care not to cut all the way through. Carefully push the stuffing into the pocket; secure the opening with toothpicks.

Heat the oil in a frying pan, add the chicken and cook until well browned on both sides. Transfer the chicken to a baking dish and bake at 400°F (200°C/Gas 6) for about 15 minutes, or until the chicken is tender. While the chicken is cooking, prepare the sauce.

Reheat the reserved bacon mixture in a pan, add the wine and stock and simmer, uncovered, until the mixture is reduced by half. Stir in the cream and blended cornstarch (cornflour) and water and stir until the sauce boils and thickens slightly. Stir in the remaining 2 teaspoons of basil.

Remove the toothpicks from the chicken and serve sliced with the sauce.

This recipe can be prepared a day ahead.

Serves 4
Preparation/Cooking Time: 1 hour 15 minutes

Port, Pear and Fig Casserole

3 tablespoons (1½ oz/45 g) butter
4 chicken legs, skin removed
4 green (spring) onions, chopped
½ cup (4 fl oz/125 ml) dry red
  wine
½ cup (4 fl oz/125 ml) port
1 cup (8 fl oz/250 ml) chicken
  stock
2 small pears, quartered
1 tablespoon plus 1 teaspoon
  cornstarch (cornflour)
1 tablespoon plus 1 teaspoon cold
  water
⅔ cup (7 oz/220 g) chunky
  cranberry sauce
4 fresh figs, quartered
1 tablespoon chopped fresh chives

Heat the butter in a large shallow frying pan, add the chicken and cook until well browned all over; remove from the pan. Drain the fat from pan, add the green (spring) onions, wine, port and stock and bring to a boil. Return the chicken and any juices accumulated from standing to the pan and simmer, covered, for 10 minutes.

Add the pears to the pan and simmer, covered, for a further 10 minutes or until tender. Blend the cornstarch (cornflour) and water and add to pears, stir until the mixture boils and thickens. Stir in the cranberry sauce, figs and chives and stir gently until hot.

Transfer to plates and serve immediately.

Serves 4
Preparation/Cooking Time: 45 minutes

Italian Boned Chicken with Pesto Mayonnaise

2 red bell peppers (capsicums)
1 (1 lb 5 oz/650 g) bunch leaf
   (English) spinach, washed
1 (3½ lbs/1.8 kg) chicken, boned
5 oz (155 g) thinly sliced mild
   salami
¼ cup (1 oz/30 g) drained
   sun-dried tomatoes, thinly sliced
5 oz (155 g) mozzarella cheese,
   grated
black pepper
1 tablespoon olive oil
1 clove garlic, crushed
string for securing

Pesto Mayonnaise:
1 cup (1 oz/30 g) lightly packed
   basil leaves
1 clove garlic, crushed
2 tablespoons grated Parmesan
   cheese
¼ cup (2 fl oz/60 ml) olive oil
½ cup (4 fl oz/125 ml) prepared
   mayonnaise
salt and pepper

Quarter the bell peppers (capsicums) and remove seeds and membranes. Broil (grill) the peppers, skin side up, until the skin blisters and blackens. Peel away the skin and cut the peppers into strips.

Boil, steam or microwave spinach until just wilted. Drain well and pat dry with paper towels.

Lightly pound the chicken to flatten. Lay the spinach leaves evenly over the chicken, top with the salami, roasted peppers, tomatoes and mozzarella cheese; sprinkle with pepper and press down firmly. Roll up tightly from the long side, tuck the ends in and continue rolling. Secure the roll with string at 1-inch (2.5-cm) intervals. Brush the roll with the combined oil and garlic. Bake at 375°F (190°C/Gas 5) for about 1 hour, or until the juices run clear when tested with a skewer. Leave to cool, then refrigerate for several hours.

Pesto Mayonnaise: Blend or process the basil, garlic, Parmesan cheese and oil until smooth. Combine the basil mixture and mayonnaise in a bowl and season with salt and pepper to taste, mixing well. Keep tightly covered until required.

Remove the string from the chicken and slice thinly. Serve with the Pesto Mayonnaise.

This recipe can be made a day ahead and the chicken roll is suitable for freezing, cooked or uncooked.

Serves 4 to 6
Preparation/Cooking Time: 2 hours

Warm Chicken and Bell Pepper Salad

2 tablespoons olive oil
1 oz (30 g) butter
4 large boneless, skinless, single
   chicken breasts
1 red bell pepper (capsicum)
1 green bell pepper (capsicum)
1 yellow bell pepper (capsicum)

Dressing:
½ cup (1¾ oz/50 g) walnuts
⅓ cup (2½ fl oz/75ml) walnut oil
¼ cup (2 fl oz/60 ml) olive oil
¼ cup (2 fl oz/60 ml) lemon juice
1 tablespoon fresh thyme leaves
1 tablespoon honey

Heat the oil and butter in a frying pan, add the chicken and cook on both sides until well browned and tender (about 10 minutes). Remove from pan, and slice.

Quarter the bell peppers and remove seeds and membranes. Grill the peppers, skin side up, until the skin blisters and blackens. Peel away skin and slice the peppers thickly.

Dressing: Combine all of the ingredients in a saucepan and stir until the honey has dissolved. (Or microwave on high [100%] power for about 1 minute.)

Arrange the chicken and peppers on plates; sprinkle with salt and pepper. Drizzle with the dressing, and serve warm.

The peppers and dressing can be prepared a day ahead.

Serves 4
Preparation/Cooking Time: 35 minutes

Greek-style Chicken Salad

4 boneless, skinless single chicken
   breasts

¼ cup (2 fl oz/60 ml) lemon juice

2 tablespoons plus ¼ cup (2 fl oz/
   60 ml) olive oil

1 tablespoon honey

2 cloves garlic, crushed

2 tablespoons chopped fresh
   rosemary

1 tablespoon grain mustard

1 medium eggplant (aubergine),
   thinly sliced

1 bunch (1 lb 5 oz/650 g) leaf
   (English) spinach

2 tomatoes, thinly sliced

1 onion, thinly sliced

¼ cup (2 oz/60 g) black (Riviera)
   olives

5 oz (155 g) feta cheese, cubed

¼ cup (2 fl oz/60 ml) extra virgin
   olive oil

Combine the chicken with the lemon juice, 2 tablespoons of the olive oil, honey, garlic, rosemary and mustard in a shallow nonmetallic dish; cover and refrigerate for several hours, or overnight. Drain the chicken from the marinade, reserve marinade.

Heat the remaining ¼ cup of olive oil in a frying pan, add the eggplant (aubergine) in batches and cook until lightly browned and tender; drain on paper towels.

Add the chicken to the frying pan and cook until well browned and tender. Take care not to burn chicken as the honey will cause it to brown quickly. Remove the chicken from the pan and slice.

Arrange the chicken, eggplant (aubergine) and remaining ingredients, except extra oil, on serving plates or bowl. Add the reserved marinade to the pan and bring to a boil. Add the extra-virgin olive oil to the marinade, spoon over the chicken and salad and serve immediately.

Serves 4
Preparation/Cooking Time: 55 minutes
Marinating Time: Several hours/overnight

Chicken and Basil Loaf with Onion–Pepper Relish

10 (approx. 8 oz/250 g) thin
   bacon strips (rashers), rind
   removed
1 onion, chopped
2 cloves garlic, crushed
½ cup (½ oz/15 g) chopped fresh
   basil
1½ lbs (750 g) ground (minced)
   chicken
2 cups (4 oz/125 g) stale
   breadcrumbs
¾ cup (6 fl oz/185 ml) heavy
   (whipping) cream
1 egg, lightly beaten
½ cup (1¾ oz/50 g) grated
   Parmesan cheese
black pepper

Onion–Pepper Relish:

3 medium red bell peppers
   (capsicums)
2 tablespoons (1 oz/30 g) butter
10 oz (315 g) small onions, sliced
   lengthwise
⅓ cup (2½ oz/75 g) superfine
   (caster) sugar
⅓ cup (3 fl oz/90 ml) dry red
   wine
2 tablespoons balsamic vinegar

Line a 9 x 5 inch (23 x 13 cm) loaf dish with 9 strips of bacon, leaving the ends of the bacon overhanging the edges of dish.

Combine the remaining loaf ingredients in a bowl and mix well. Press the mixture firmly into the prepared dish. Fold the overhanging bacon over the mixture and lay the remaining strip of bacon along the center. Cover the dish with foil and place in a baking dish with enough boiling water to come halfway up the sides of the dish. Bake at 350°F (180°C/Gas 4) for about 1½ hours, or until firm. Cool slightly, and pour off any liquid that has accumulated on top of the loaf. Turn out and slice.

Onion–Pepper Relish: Quarter the bell peppers, and remove seeds and membranes. Broil (grill) the peppers, skin side up, for about 10 minutes, or until the skin blisters and blackens. Peel the skin away and slice the peppers thinly.

Heat the butter in a saucepan, add the onions and cook, covered, over low heat for about 10 minutes, or until soft. Add the remaining ingredients and peppers and simmer, uncovered, for about 15 minutes, or until most of the liquid has evaporated.

Serve the Chicken and Basil Loaf warm or cold with the Onion–Pepper Relish.

This recipe can be made up to two days ahead. Store the loaf and relish separately in the refrigerator. Any leftover loaf is also delicious as a sandwich filling.

Serves 6
Preparation/Cooking Time: 2 hours

Smoked Cheese and Chicken Roll

4 tablespoons (2 oz/60 g) butter

⅓ cup (1¾ oz/50 g) all-purpose
(plain) flour

1 cup (8 fl oz/250 ml) milk

1 cup (3 oz/90 g) grated smoked
cheese

4 eggs, separated

Chicken Filling:

3 tablespoons (1½ oz/45 g) butter

10 oz (315 g) mushrooms, finely
chopped

4 green (spring) onions, chopped

2 cloves garlic, crushed

¼ cup (2 fl oz/60 ml) sour cream

8 oz (250 g) cooked chicken, finely
chopped

Lightly grease a 10½ x 13 in (26 x 32 cm) jelly roll pan (Swiss roll tin), line the base and 2 opposite sides with parchment (non-stick baking) paper.

Heat the butter in a saucepan, add the flour and cook, stirring, until dry and grainy (about 1 minute). Remove from the heat and gradually stir in the milk, return to the heat and stir until the mixture boils and thickens. Stir in the cheese and egg yolks.

Beat the egg whites in a small bowl with an electric mixer until soft peaks form, gently fold into the cheese mixture in 2 batches. Pour into the prepared pan and spread gently. Bake at 450°F (230°C/Gas 8) for about 15 minutes or until puffed and firm to the touch. Meanwhile, prepare the filling.

Filling: Heat the butter in a frying pan, add the mushrooms and cook, stirring, until the mushrooms are soft and the excess liquid has evaporated. Add the green (spring) onions and garlic, cook, stirring, until the onions are soft. Add the sour cream and chicken and stir until well combined. Do not allow to boil.

When roll is cooked, remove from oven and run a knife around the edge of the pan and then invert the pan onto a clean tea towel. Remove the lining paper and quickly spread with the filling. Roll up firmly from the short side. Let stand, covered with the tea towel, for 5 minutes. Serve sliced.

This recipe can be made a day ahead and served cold.

Serves 4 to 6 as an appetizer
Preparation/Cooking Time: 1 hour

Spiced Lime Chicken Salad

2 tablespoons vegetable oil

6 boneless, skinless, single chicken breasts

1 tablespoon ground cumin

2 carrots

7 oz (220 g) fresh asparagus, chopped

7 oz (220 g) sugar snap peas

1 red bell pepper (capsicum), thinly sliced

5 oz (155 g) bean sprouts

1 head romaine (Cos) lettuce, washed and torn

1 onion, thinly sliced and washed

Dressing:

¾ cup (6 fl oz/185 ml) vegetable oil

1 teaspoon grated lime zest

½ cup (4 fl oz/125 ml) lime juice

¼ cup (¼ oz/7.5 g) chopped fresh coriander (cilantro)

2 teaspoons chopped fresh chili pepper

2 tablespoons Thai fish sauce

1 tablespoon sugar

3 cloves garlic, crushed

2 tablespoons chopped fresh mint

Heat the oil in a frying pan. Sprinkle the chicken with cumin, add to the pan and cook until the chicken is well browned and tender. Remove from the pan and cut into thick slices.

Peel the carrots lengthways into strips with a vegetable peeler and place in a bowl of cold water until crisp (about 30 minutes). Boil, steam or microwave the asparagus and peas until just tender, drain, refresh in iced water and drain again.

Dressing: Combine all ingredients in a screw-top jar and shake well.

Combine the warm chicken with the vegetables, sprouts, lettuce and onion in a bowl and toss well. Drizzle with dressing just before serving.

Serves 6
Preparation/Cooking Time: 40 minutes

Roasted Garlic Chicken with Goat Cheese Bruschetta

1 (3½ lb/1.8 kg) chicken
2 sprigs fresh rosemary
2 sprigs fresh thyme
1 lb (500 g) heads (bulbs) garlic
¼ cup (2 fl oz/60 ml) olive oil
2 tablespoons (1 oz/30 g) butter,
    melted
salt and black pepper

Goat Cheese Bruschetta:

1 large French baguette
¼ cup (2 fl oz/60 ml) olive oil
2 tablespoons olive paste or pâté
2 tablespoons sun-dried tomato
    paste or pâté
3½ oz (100 g) goat cheese,
    crumbled
1 tablespoon chopped fresh thyme

Trim excess fat from the chicken, rinse and pat dry. Place the herbs in the cavity of the chicken. Tie the chicken legs together, tuck the wings under the body. Break the garlic into cloves — do not peel. Place the chicken in a baking dish and put the garlic around the chicken. Brush the chicken with half the combined oil and butter and drizzle the remainder over the garlic. Sprinkle the chicken and garlic with salt and pepper. Roast in a moderate oven (375°F/190°C/Gas 5) for about 1¾ hours, or until chicken is tender; stir the garlic occasionally.

Goat Cheese Bruschetta: Slice the bread diagonally into ½ inch (1.25 cm) thick slices — you will need about 16 slices. Lightly brush both sides of the bread with oil and broil (grill) on one side until lightly browned. Spread half the slices with olive paste and half with sun-dried tomato paste. Sprinkle with the goat cheese and thyme and broil (grill) until lightly browned.

When the chicken is cooked, remove from the oven and leave to stand for five minutes. Remove the string and serve the chicken, drizzled with pan juices, and the bruschetta immediately.

Serves 6
Preparation/Cooking Time: 2 hours 40 minutes

Creamy Chicken and Leek Pie

2 cups (8 oz/250 g) all-purpose
  (plain) flour
5 oz (155 g) cream cheese, chopped
6 tablespoons (3 oz/90 g) butter,
  chopped
3 egg yolks
1 tablespoon water, approximately
2 teaspoons water, extra

Filling:
1 tablespoon vegetable oil
1½ lbs (750 g) boneless, skinless
  chicken breasts, chopped
2 leeks, sliced and well washed
3 bacon strips (rashers), chopped
2 cloves garlic, crushed
3 tablespoons (1½ oz/45 g) butter
2 tablespoons all-purpose (plain)
  flour
½ cup (4 fl oz/125 ml) dry white
  wine
1 cup (8 fl oz/250 ml) milk
⅓ cup (1½ oz/45 g) grated
  cheddar cheese
⅓ cup (1 oz/30 g) grated
  Parmesan cheese
2 teaspoons grain mustard
1 tablespoon chopped fresh thyme
salt and pepper

Sift the flour into a bowl, rub in the cream cheese and the butter. Add two egg yolks and about 1 tablespoon of water. Mix. Knead pastry until smooth, cover and refrigerate for 30 minutes.

Lightly grease a 9–10 inch (22.5–25 cm) pie dish. Divide the dough in half, roll one half large enough to line the bottom and sides of the pie dish; trim the edges. Cover the pastry with foil or parchment paper and fill with dried beans or rice. Bake at 400°F (200°C/Gas 6) for 15 minutes. Remove the paper and beans and bake for a further 10 minutes, or until the pastry is lightly browned. Cool.

Filling: Heat the oil in a frying pan, add the chicken in batches and cook, stirring, until browned; remove from pan. Reheat the pan, add the leeks, bacon and garlic and cook, stirring, until the leeks are soft. Add the butter and flour and cook, stirring, until the liquid is bubbling. Remove from the heat and gradually add the wine and milk. Place back on the heat and cook, stirring, until the mixture boils and thickens. Stir in the cheeses, mustard, thyme and chicken; mix well and season with salt and pepper. Leave to cool slightly.

Spoon the filling into the pastry shell. Combine remaining egg yolk with 2 teaspoons of water, brush onto the edges of the pastry shell. Roll out the second half of the dough until it is large enough to fit over the top of the pie. Cover the pie and press the edges together firmly, trim the edges and pinch a decorative frill around them. Brush the pastry with more egg yolk mixture and decorate with pastry leaves. Cut two slits in the pastry. Bake at 400°F (200°C/Gas 6) for about 35 minutes, or until the pie is golden brown and hot.

Serves 6 to 8
Preparation Time: 50 minutes
Resting and Cooking Time: 1 hour 30 minutes

Chicken with Couscous, Chick Peas and Cumin Sauce

1 (3½ lb/1.8 kg) chicken
2 tablespoons (1 oz/30 g) butter, melted
1 teaspoon ground cumin
2 teaspoons cumin seed
2 cups (16 fl oz/500 ml) chicken stock
1 tablespoon plus 1 teaspoon honey
harissa, for serving

Couscous:
2 cups (12 oz/375 g) couscous
1½ cups (12 fl oz/375 ml) boiling water
8 tablespoons (4 oz/125 g) butter
1 onion, chopped
2 cloves garlic, crushed
2 teaspoons cumin seed
2 teaspoons coriander (cilantro) seed
1 teaspoon chopped fresh chili pepper
½ teaspoon ground cinnamon
pinch saffron
2 tablespoons currants
1 (13 oz/410 g) can chick peas (garbanzo beans), rinsed and drained

Tie the legs of the chicken together, tuck the wings under the body. Place the chicken on a wire rack in a baking dish, brush with melted butter and sprinkle with cumin. Pour ½ cup water into the dish and bake at 350°F (180°C/Gas 4) for about 1¾ hours, or until golden brown and tender.

Couscous: Put the couscous in a bowl and pour over the boiling water. Let stand for 2 to 3 minutes, or until the water is absorbed.

Heat the butter in a frying pan, add the onion, garlic, seeds, chili pepper and spices and cook, stirring, until the onion is soft. Add the couscous, currants and chick peas (garbanzo beans) and cook, stirring, until well combined and heated through.

When the chicken is cooked, remove from oven. Drain the fat from the dish, heat the remaining juices, stirring, until well browned. Then add the cumin seeds and cook, stirring, until fragrant. Add the stock and honey and simmer, uncovered, for about 2 minutes, scraping the base of the pan. Strain the sauce, serve with the chicken, couscous and harissa.

The couscous can be made a day ahead. Harissa is a hot Tunisian chili sauce that is usually available from Middle Eastern stores.

Serves 4 to 6
Preparation/Cooking Time: 2 hours 30 minutes

Blackened Chicken
with Chili–Tomato Coulis

Chili–Tomato Coulis:

⅓ cup (2.5 fl oz/75 ml) tomato sauce (purée)

1 tomato, finely chopped

1 tablespoon plus 1 teaspoon lime juice

1 tablespoon plus 1 teaspoon chili sauce

¼ teaspoon Tabasco sauce

½ teaspoon salt

2 teaspoons chopped fresh dill

pepper to taste

6 boneless, skinless, single chicken breasts

1 tablespoon plus 1 teaspoon paprika

2 teaspoons black pepper

approx. ½ teaspoon cayenne pepper

2 teaspoons garlic powder

2 teaspoons onion powder

1 teaspoon salt

1 teaspoon dried thyme

8 tablespoons (4 oz/125 g) butter, melted

Chili–Tomato Coulis: Combine all of the ingredients in a bowl; mix well. Stand for at least 1 hour.

Pound the chicken breasts lightly until thinner and of an even thickness.

Combine the dry ingredients in a screw-top jar, using more cayenne if a hotter mix is required; shake well. Heat barbecue or cast-iron skillet or grill pan for about 10 minutes, until very hot.

Dip the chicken into melted butter and sprinkle the spice mixture on both sides. Cook the chicken for about 2 minutes on each side, until a black crust forms and the chicken is cooked through. (This cooking process will create a lot of smoke and is best done outdoors. Have a strong exhaust fan operating if cooking indoors.)

Serve the chicken with Tomato–Chili Sauce and some extra melted butter, if desired.

The spice mix can be made several weeks ahead. Store in an airtight jar at room temperature. The sauce can be made a day ahead.

Serves 6
Preparation/Cooking Time: 30 minutes
Standing Time: 1 hour

Olive–Seasoned Chicken with Roasted Tomatoes and Onions

1 (3½ lb/1.8 kg) chicken

6 tablespoons (3 oz/90 g) butter, softened

½ cup (3½ oz/100 g) finely chopped pitted black olives

4 cloves garlic, crushed

black pepper

12 (about 10 oz/315 g) baby onions, peeled

8 oz (250 g) red cherry tomatoes

8 oz (250 g) yellow pear (teardrop) tomatoes

½ cup (½ oz/15 g) lightly packed whole basil leaves

Carefully loosen the chicken breast skin. Beat the butter, olives and garlic in a bowl with a wooden spoon until combined. Spoon the mixture under the skin of the chicken, and ease evenly over the flesh using your hands. Tie the chicken legs together and tuck the wings under the body. Sprinkle the chicken with pepper and place in a baking dish. Roast at 400°F (200°C/Gas 6) for 45 minutes.

Add the onions to the pan, turning them to coat in the pan juices; roast for a further 30 minutes. Add the tomatoes and basil and roast for a further 15 minutes, or until the chicken is tender.

Remove the chicken from the oven and leave to stand for 5 minutes, then remove the string. Serve the chicken with the onions, tomatoes and basil. Drizzle with some of the pan juices, if desired.

The chicken can be prepared up to a day ahead, but is best cooked close to serving.

If yellow pear (teardrop) tomatoes are unavailable, use red cherry tomatoes only. The chicken is also delicious served cold on bread rolls or as a sandwich.

Serves 4 to 6
Preparation/Cooking Time: 2 hours

Hearty Chicken Casserole with Rye and Raisin Bread

Rye and Raisin Bread:

1 cup (5 oz/155 g) whole wheat (wholemeal plain) flour

1 cup (5 oz/155 g) rye flour

1 teaspoon baking soda

1¼ cups cornmeal

1 tablespoon sugar

¼ cup chopped raisins

1½ cups (12 fl oz/375 ml) milk

½ cup (4 fl oz/125 ml) molasses

1 teaspoon malt (brown) vinegar

2 tablespoons vegetable oil

4 lbs (2 kg) cut-up chicken pieces

2 onions, sliced lengthwise

2 cloves garlic, crushed

½ lb (250 g) speck or prosciutto

3 carrots, thickly sliced

2 stalks celery, thickly sliced

1 (14 oz/440 g) can tomatoes

⅓ cup (2.5 fl oz/85 ml) tomato paste

1 cup (8 fl oz/250 ml) chicken stock

1 (1 lb/500 g) can cannellini beans, rinsed, drained

⅓ cup (⅓ oz/10 g) chopped basil

2 tablespoons chopped oregano

Rye and Raisin Bread: Lightly grease 9 x 5 inch (23 x 13 cm) loaf pan, line the base with paper, then grease the paper.

Combine the dry ingredients in a bowl, then stir in the raisins, milk, molasses and vinegar. Spoon the mixture into the prepared pan and bake at 375°F (190°C/Gas 5) for about 50 minutes, or until a skewer inserted in the middle comes out clean.

Let stand for 5 minutes then turn onto a wire rack to cool. While the bread is baking, prepare the chicken casserole.

Heat the oil in a large wide pan, add the chicken pieces in batches and cook over a high heat until well browned all over. Remove the chicken to a plate. Add the onions, garlic, thinly sliced speck, carrots and celery to the pan and cook, stirring, until the onions are soft. Add the undrained crushed tomatoes, tomato paste and stock and bring to a boil. Return the chicken pieces to the pan and simmer, uncovered, for about 15 minutes, or until the chicken is just tender. Add the beans and herbs, and simmer until heated through.

Serve with slices of Rye and Raisin Bread and butter.

This recipe can be made a day ahead and is also suitable for freezing.

Serves 6
Preparation/Cooking Time: 1 hour 50 minutes

Barbecued Cornish Game Hens and Vegetables with Aïoli

2 x 1 lb 14 oz (900 g) Cornish
  game hens (or baby chickens)
½ cup (4 fl oz/125 ml) olive oil
¼ cup (2 fl oz/60 ml) lemon juice
2 cloves garlic, crushed
4 green (spring) onions, chopped
1 tablespoon chopped fresh thyme
4 thin Oriental (lady finger)
  eggplants (aubergines)
2 zucchinis (courgettes)
2 yellow squash zucchinis
  (courgettes)
2 red bell peppers (capsicums)
4 medium red-skinned potatoes
coarse salt
freshly ground black pepper

Aïoli:
2 egg yolks
¼ teaspoon salt
2 cloves garlic, crushed
⅔ cup (5 fl oz/155 ml) vegetable
  oil
⅓ cup (2½ fl oz/75 ml) olive oil
1 tablespoon lemon juice

Using poultry shears or a sharp knife, cut along either side of the backbones of the chickens. Remove and discard backbones. Place the chickens, breast-side up, on a work surface, and flatten with your hand. Combine the oil, lemon juice, garlic, green (spring) onions and thyme and brush the chickens with some of this mixture. Cook on a covered barbecue over a very low heat, for about 30 minutes, or until almost tender, turning once during cooking. (If you do not have a barbecue with a cover for slow cooking, bake the chickens at 375°F (190°C/Gas 5) for about 30 minutes, or until almost tender. Finish the chickens on a barbecue to brown and produce a smoky flavor.)

Aïoli: Blend or process the egg yolks, salt and garlic until smooth. Gradually add the oils in a thin stream, with motor running, until the mixture is thick. Transfer to a bowl and stir in the lemon juice.

Thinly slice the eggplants (aubergines) and the zucchinis (courgettes) lengthways. Cut the bell peppers (capsicums) into thick strips; thinly slice the potatoes. Brush the vegetables with some of the oil mixture and barbecue beside the chickens until well browned and tender (about 10 minutes). Drizzle with the remaining oil mixture and serve with salt, pepper and Aïoli.

Serves 4 to 6
Preparation/Cooking Time: 1 hour 10 minutes

Wild Rice Seasoned Chicken with Grand Marnier Glaze

Seasoning:

½ cup (3½ oz/100 g) wild rice
1 tablespoon vegetable oil
1 onion, chopped
1 clove garlic, crushed
1 stalk celery, chopped
¼ cup (¾ oz/20 g) chopped fresh
  chives
½ cup (1 oz/30 g) stale
  breadcrumbs
½ cup (1¾ oz/50 g) chopped
  pecans
1 egg, lightly beaten
salt and pepper

1 (3½ lb/1.8 kg) chicken
1 tablespoon orange marmalade
1 tablespoon Grand Marnier
  liqueur

Basting Sauce:

¾ cup (6 fl oz/185 ml) dry white
  wine
¼ cup (2 oz/60 g) orange
  marmalade
1 tablespoon plus 1 teaspoon
  cornstarch (cornflour)
1 cup (8 fl oz/250 ml) orange
  juice
2 teaspoons Grand Marnier

Seasoning: Add the wild rice to a saucepan of boiling water and cook, uncovered, for 20 to 30 minutes, or until rice is just tender; drain.

Heat the oil in a saucepan, add the onion, garlic and celery and cook, stirring, until the onion is soft; cool. Combine the wild rice and onion mixture with the remaining ingredients in a bowl and mix well.

Fill the chicken cavity with the seasoning; tie the legs together and tuck the wings under body. Place the chicken on a wire rack in a baking dish, pour ¼ cup water into the dish. Roast, uncovered, at 400°F (200°C/Gas 6) for 1 hour.

After the chicken has roasted for an hour, brush it with the combined marmalade and Grand Marnier and roast for a further 30 minutes, or until tender.

Basting Sauce: Combine the wine, marmalade and cornstarch (cornflour) and ¼ cup of the orange juice in a saucepan; stir until the mixture boils and thickens. Stir in the remaining orange juice and Grand Marnier and keep stirring until hot.

When the chicken is cooked, let stand for 5 minutes, then remove string. Serve with the sauce.

The seasoning and sauce can be prepared a day ahead.

Serves 6
Preparation/Cooking Time: 2 hours 40 minutes

Chicken Antipasto Platter

6 tablespoons (3½ fl oz/100 ml)
  olive oil

1 tablespoon balsamic vinegar

2 tablespoons chopped fresh basil

2 cloves garlic, crushed

6 boneless, skinless, single chicken
  breasts, sliced lengthwise in
  strips

2 x 6 oz (185 g) jars marinated
  artichoke hearts

3 oz (90 g) small white (button)
  mushrooms

4 oz (125 g) black olives

3 oz (90 g) bocconcini
  (mozzarella balls), drained

12 baby radishes, trimmed

¼ cup (4 oz/125 g) homemade or
  store-bought pesto

2 loaves focaccia, sliced into
  wedges*

Italian bread (Grissini) sticks

*Any crusty Italian bread could
  be used in this recipe.

This recipe is pictured on page 3.

Combine 5 tablespoons of the oil with the vinegar, basil and garlic; mix well.

Heat the remaining 1 tablespoon of oil in a frying pan, add the chicken and cook, stirring, until the chicken is tender. Pour ¼ cup of the oil mixture over the chicken, cool and then refrigerate for several hours.

Combine the artichoke hearts and mushrooms in a bowl and pour on the remaining oil mixture. Cover and refrigerate for several hours.

Arrange the chicken, artichokes, mushrooms, olives, bocconcini, radishes and pesto on a platter. Toast the focaccia until it is lightly browned, spread with some pesto. Serve with bread sticks and platter.

This recipe can be prepared up to a day ahead.

Serves 4 to 6 as a light lunch or appetizer
Preparation/Cooking Time: 35 minutes